W9-BMO-183

Investigating Institutional Racism

A. Rochaun
Meadows-Fernandez

Enslow Publishing
101 W. 23rd Street
Suite 240
New York, NY 10011
USA

enslow.com

Published in 2019 by Enslow Publishing, LLC.
101 W. 23rd Street, Suite 240, New York, NY 10011

Library of Congress Cataloging-in-Publication Data

Names: Meadows-Fernandez, A. Rochaun, author.
Title: Investigating institutional racism / A. Rochaun Meadows-Fernandez.
Description: New York, NY : Enslow Publishing, 2019. | Series: Racial literacy | Audience: Grades 7–12. | Includes bibliographical references and index.
Identifiers: LCCN 2018018854| ISBN 9781978504707 (library bound) | ISBN 9781978505650 (pbk.)
Subjects: LCSH: Racism—United States. | United States—Race relations.
Classification: LCC E184.A1 M358 2019 | DDC 305.800973—dc23
LC record available at https://lccn.loc.gov/2018018854

Printed in the United States of America

To Our Readers: We have done our best to make sure all website addresses in this book were active and appropriate when we went to press. However, the author and the publisher have no control over and assume no liability for the material available on those websites or on any websites they may link to. Any comments or suggestions can be sent by e-mail to customerservice@enslow.com.

Photo Credits: Cover, p. 1 Bim/E+Getty Images; p. 5 © North Wind Picture Archives; p. 6 Transcendental Graphics/Archive Photos/Getty Images; p. 9 adamkaz/Vetta/Getty Images; pp. 11, 15, 21, 27, 36, 40 © AP Images; p. 13 Ross Petukhov/Shutterstock.com; p. 16 Julie Dermansky/Corbis News/Getty Images; p. 17 Portland Press Herald/Getty Images; p. 18 Bill Pugliano/Getty Images; p. 23 Baltimore Sun/Tribune News Service/Getty Images; p. 28 David Portnoy/Getty Images; p. 30 Chester Brown/Alamy Stock Photo; p. 32 Viviane Moos/Corbis Historical/Getty Images; p. 34 The Washington Post/Getty Images; p. 38 Photo 12/Universal Images Group/Getty Images; p. 42 Giles Clarke/Getty Images; p. 46 Aleutie/Shutterstock.com; p. 48 Witthaya Prasongsin/Moment/Getty Images; p. 50 Monkey Business Images/Shutterstock.com; p. 51 Onoky Photononstop/Alamy Stock Photo; pp. 53, 67 Andrey_Popov/Shutterstock.com; p. 54 Yeexin Richelle/Shutterstock.com; p. 56 Boston Globe/Getty Images; p. 57 Hulton Archive/Getty Images; p. 59 Darren Baker/Shutterstock.com; p. 61 Pacific Press/LightRocket/Getty Images; p. 64 Win McNamee/Getty Images; p. 65 Andrew Lichtenstein/Corbis News/Getty Images; p. 66 Rawpixel.com/Shutterstock.com; cover and interior pages background design Ensuper/Shutterstock.com (colors), Miloje/Shutterstock.com (texture).

C O N T E N T S

Introduction

Before we can talk about racism, we must talk about race. It's confusing, messy, and more important, a social construct. Race is the idea that differences in the way we look, like skin color and hair texture, tell us about deeper differences like intelligence, behavioral patterns, and the likelihood of committing a crime.

In the United States, the use of racial hierarchies with white people at the top was created to justify the land theft from and genocide of Native populations, along with the dehumanization of African slaves to justify slavery. Since then, Americans have been labeled white or "other" and treated accordingly. America's systems were developed for the benefit of white Americans. Immediately after slavery, many Black Americans did work that closely resembled slave labor, as sharecroppers. Similarly, Jim Crow laws maintained Black Americans' exclusion from the education system, employment industry, and access to the health care for many years afterward.

George Washington is shown walking through a field with his slaves in the surrounding area.

Racism is a math problem: Prejudice plus systemic power equals institutional racism. Systemic power is the ability to control systems like education, health care, media, and employment to the benefit of one group over others. While racism looks like different things to different people on an individual level, institutional racism is the bigger structural social framework that promotes racial discrimination. If individual racism is the school bully, then institutional racism is when the teacher hates you, too, and praises the bully while handing you unearned detention.

Institutional racism can also look like oversimplifying several distinct ethnic groups by reducing their variety of social and cultural traditions into one homogenous group. For example, in the United States there are 562 legally recognized Native tribes with individual languages, cultures, and customs. Unfortunately, social and cultural institutions often discuss them as one. There is a similar issue with Hispanic/Latinx people and Asians. The social construction of race forces oversimplifying race and ethnicity. It's not just black and white. It's important to note that you can be Asian and Latinx or Latinx and Native or Latinx and Black or

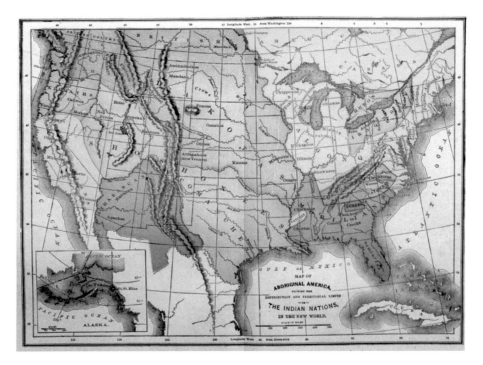

Our nation looked different two hundred years ago. Above is a map of Aboriginal America, showing some of the Native American tribes in 1870.

any combination of the three. Whether you are white, Black, Native, Latinx, or Asian will have an effect on your life and access to opportunities.

Institutional racism is all around us but is especially present in education, media, employment, the criminal justice system, and health care.

CHAPTER 1

What Is Institutional Racism?

Racism can show up in many ways. Sometimes it is easy to spot, like with stereotypes and bullying. But other times, racism is hidden in policies that target characteristics thought to help predict race, like income levels, names, and neighborhoods.

Individual Racism

Individual racism is the harmful things people say or do that are related to someone else's racial category. However, racism is much more complex than making mean comments and explicit exclusion. Another form of individual racism, also referred to as benevolent racism, is based on the idea that Black Americans and other minorities are incompetent and require white sympathy and assistance for success.

Bullying is a major problem in schools and should never be accepted.

Racism might look like a teacher or a student making a Black or Brown kid feel like their culture isn't OK to show in school. If a teacher tells an Arab American student that they cannot wear a hijab in their classroom because the teacher doesn't like it, it's individual racism.

Institutional Racism

But institutional racism is when the systems in place, such as education, criminal justice, and health care, exclude or harm people of color. For example, a Black student was given a three-day suspension and a fine for standing up to a bully, but the white bully was given the chance to apologize and return to class—this is institutional racism.

Many individuals who carried personal prejudices and racist views wanted to do what they could to make sure things functioned like they did during the years after slavery—they wanted their neighborhoods and schools to stay white. The Civil Rights Act of 1964 helped to punish people for obvious acts of race-based discrimination in areas like employment and education.[1] However, it could not stop less direct discrimination, like name screening for race, or change the prejudice that led people to discriminate in the first place.

Our government agencies and institutions realized that there were ways to exclude Black people without saying "No Blacks need apply" like in the old days. These mindsets were used to develop policies and procedures that indirectly affected people of color.[2]

This method of taking hateful mindsets and indoctrinating them into larger systems' functioning is referred to as institutional racism. The institutions of education, wealth, media, criminal justice, and health are independent yet interactive. This means that if a person of color is able to move to a "rich" neighborhood, they can still be targeted by the criminal justice system, shown as a thug in the media, and treated badly by health care professionals. We can see this in the way Black athletes, like Serena Williams, are subjected to racist comments, despite having money and global success.[3]

But at the same time, a poor person of color can deal with the compound effects of having no money to get to work, no access to a higher education, struggling to find a job that provides a livable wage, and trouble with law enforcement.

Elizabeth Eckford, one of the Little Rock Nine, is verbally assaulted while walking into Central High School on September 4, 1957.

The Elephant in the Room

Race is always the elephant in the room. Some people think by avoiding certain words, we can avoid discussing race and reducing racial profiling. But race is everywhere. Although most experts agree race is a social construct and our differences have no real biological grounding, race still affects us—a lot.

Since 2016, the rate for hate crimes has risen roughly 16 percent, with a particular increase in anti-Muslim crimes. If you don't think racism exists, that might be pretty shocking.

In the United States, there are huge racial differences in views of racial inequality. Only 53 percent of white Americans believe we still have work to do to achieve racial equality. In contrast, 88 percent of Black Americans believe we need to do more to reach equality. Similarly, 61 percent of Blacks say race relations are bad compared to 45 percent of whites.[2] How can two groups of people who live in the same areas report such different perspectives? Perhaps it's because they use different measuring tools.

Colorblind Racism

In the last few decades, colorblind racism has emerged because many people refuse to talk about the realities of racial prejudice. Colorblindness is the idea that we are all the same and if we ignore race, we will live in a happy world. Calling social programs like affirmative action, which were created in hopes of leveling the playing field for people of color, unfair to white people is an example of colorblind racism. Saying we should ignore race implies that racial discrimination has ended. This requires denying the experiences of racial discrimination that people of color report every day and saying we have already reached racial equality. The problem with this is by ignoring race altogether, we overlook the harm that has been done to people of color in America's history. As a result, we miss opportunities to change individual and institutional racism.

Data shows hiring biases of the past are still alive and well despite attempts at their reduction. Racial discrimination is a serious obstacle for people of color seeking employment.

Black Americans, and other minority groups, look at race and racism through the lens of their experiences with education, employment, and the criminal justice system. White America often discusses race through a lens of individually racist acts and legal change.

It's important to study all forms of racism in hopes that we eventually will achieve racial equity—a reality where your race doesn't change how likely you are to experience privileges or disadvantages in a racially-based society. Institutional racism stops people of color from being treated as equals to white people, and this causes problems in health, wealth, and other institutions.

CHAPTER 2

Education

The year 2013 was a bad year for Black girls with natural hair. After being teased for wearing her hair naturally, twelve-year-old Vanessa VanDyke was given a week to straighten her hair or be expelled from her school, Faith Christian Academy in Orlando, Florida.[1] According to her school's dress code, "Hair must be a natural color and must not be a distraction" and goes on to state examples that include, but are not limited to, mohawks, shaved designs, and rat tails. VanDyke's hair was considered a distraction.

This phenomenon of policing Black girls' hair includes seven-year-old Tiana Parker having to change schools because she had dreadlocks, which, according to Deborah Brown Community School in Tulsa, Oklahoma, was both "faddish" and "unacceptable" and "distract from the respectful and serious atmosphere it strives for."[2,3]

In 2014, hair discrimination continued when five-year-old Malachi Wilson was sent home from school for his long hair, despite haircuts being against his religious beliefs as a member of the Navajo Nation.[4]

Tiana Parker, seven, featured above with her family, was pulled out of school after she was told that her dreadlocks violated the dress code at Deborah Brown Community School.

Too often, white standards of acceptable beauty and behavior are used to develop school regulations that unfairly target children of color. In this way, children of color in the school system have their cultures criminalized, and it leads to further exclusion from education. Unfortunately, this is just one of many ways the education system disproportionally lets down Black and Brown children.

This information paints a picture that children of color have additional obstacles. Things like access to a quality education, funding, standardized tests, and college readiness are often developed without considering the unique experiences of children of color. To illustrate this, we are going to look at the condition of schools in Detroit, Michigan.

Access to a Quality Education

Detroit's education system has been in the news a lot lately—for all the wrong reasons. It's an area overwhelmingly represented by people of color, and the schools are all but closed. Some of the details are downright shocking: In 2016, they were still using textbooks from 1995.[5] Many classrooms lacked air conditioning. Some class sizes were as large as 50 students, and there was even an instance of an eighth grader having to instruct the seventh and eighth graders' math class for a month.

While Detroit schools are extreme examples, they serve as reminders that children of color have issues accessing a quality education.[6]

Many schools in Detroit were abandoned after a troubled economy led to widespread bankruptcy.

Where's the Money?

More than half of Detroit's students live in poverty, and their education quality reflects it.[7] They have some of the lowest test scores in the nation, a severe teacher shortage, and their facilities are a risk to public health.

Public schools are mostly funded by property taxes. Neighborhoods with wealthier families and higher-cost homes have more money to spend in their school districts, while areas that have mostly apartment complexes like lower-income neighborhoods only receive money from the government.

People of color don't often choose to live in areas with little to no property value that lead to less funding for their children. Institutional racism has led to limited access to high-paying jobs and less disposable income. Institutional racism creates a vicious cycle: Black and Brown families live in areas with low-performing schools that lack up–to-date textbooks and focus on limiting behavioral issues instead of teaching children. As a result, the students don't learn enough to get into college. Most good jobs require college degrees, so these children end up in low-skilled jobs and neighborhoods similar to where they grew up. This is called the cycle of poverty.

Outdated textbooks are a common feature in Detroit schools.

Teacher Quality

The teachers employed in low-income districts often have less experience than those in more affluent and less diverse districts.[8] Additionally, if a local school is underperforming, white children are more likely to have the means to travel to another district or attend private school.

Since many teachers in low-income schools have standard teaching degrees, it's not uncommon for one instructor to have to teach several unrelated subjects. Because these teachers don't have the detailed knowledge and background in these other subjects they are forced to teach, their students will not receive a well-rounded education.

Detroit teachers protest for fair pay and treatment. Similar teacher protests are occurring around the nation.

Research suggests children of color do better in school when they have a teacher and curriculum that understand their cultural circumstances.[9] However, for many students of color having teachers who are from a perspective that acknowledges their cultural lifestyle and teach materials in a way they can relate to is rare. Because of institutional racism, few youth of color have the education or the funds to complete competitive teaching programs and become teachers themselves.

Another obstacle is that teachers of color might not be seen as a good fit because the way they talk or wear their hair doesn't match with what schools see as "professional." The result is fewer teachers of color.

Who Sets the Standard for Standardized Tests?

Standardized tests are one of many ways youth of color and their schools are left out of the system. The people who create the tests children of color take are typically white, female, and middle class. This causes the test to be written from a perspective that many Black and Brown youth cannot relate to. So, how does this affect them?

The tests that are used to measure a student's success during school are also those that are used when it's time to graduate. Many of the words children are expected to know to show they're ready for college are based on the culture and customs of white Americans. Additionally, the answers to standardized tests aren't based on "common sense" or traditional knowledge.[10] Instead, they are based on the information in textbooks. Since many districts in low-income schools don't have access to the textbooks referenced by test writers, they don't have access to the correct answers. Sadly, many low-income districts don't have the means to provide every student with a textbook, let alone take them home. Imagine how hard that makes it to study for a test.

Because a school's job is judged by standardized test scores, lower test results lead to closing schools. And because low-income school districts have less access to materials that would raise test scores, these students often get left behind. For many children of color, the education system is one of their first experiences with institutional racism.

Achievement Gap

The achievement gap is a term for the differences in grades, dropout rates, standardized-test scores, course options, and college success experienced by different students.

Black and Brown youth are often behind in their math and reading skills, sometimes as much as thirty points larger than in 1992, and one of the biggest reasons is lack of quality education access.[11] Lower reading and math scores put children of color at a heightened risk for being held back or not graduating at all. An estimated 12 percent of Hispanic students drop out of high school. Like other students of color who drop out, this happens for a variety of reasons including that they lack support and occasionally because they have had to take on responsibilities of solving problems at home.[12] Many children of color who struggle in school report not feeling supported, and some even suggested their instructors expressed an expectation that they would not finish school.[13]

Private and magnet schools yield better outcomes but are often inaccessible due to cost or location for children of color. Still, magnet schools are not a fix-all solution for institutional racism in education. In Connecticut, eight parents of color are suing the local district because the local magnet school is limited to 75 percent minority attendance.[14] Because white students do not want to attend this magnet school, 25 percent of the desks remain empty and access to those classes are closed to other qualified students of color.

Chris Frank, director of the Magnet Program at Northeast High School, spoke with students to provide insight into the available charter and private schools for Philadelphia's elementary students.

Other places don't have quotas, like the top-performing schools in New Orleans, but they have other barriers.[15] Of students in New Orleans, 84 percent in public schools are low-income and the extensive paperwork, far distances from their homes, and frequent parent-teacher meetings may not be feasible for low-income and single minority parents hoping for their kids to attend these schools.

Punishment

In 2013, Parkland shooter Nikolas Cruz had twenty-six disciplinary incidents.[16] He was suspended for fighting, reported to law enforcement several times, and even alleged on social media that he had intentions to shoot up a school a year before the event took place.[17] Cruz, like many other troubled white students, had been disciplined via suspension several times. But after repeated run-ins was never seen as enough of a threat for further action.

Compare Cruz's experience with that of Ryan Turk at Graham Park Middle School in Virginia.[18] In 2016, Turk was handcuffed for stealing milk despite the fact he gets a free lunch and the milk was included. Naturally, he resisted the officer and was later suspended for theft, being disrespectful, and using his cell phone in school. He was also charged with larceny and ordered to appear in court. Institutional racism makes first-time offenders of color more likely to get criminal records than repeat white offenders.

Children of color, and Black children especially, are more likely to be suspended, expelled, and sent to in-school detention than other children. As early as kindergarten, Black children are four times more likely to be suspended.[19] When comparing the rates, Black boys, closely followed by Black girls, are punished more frequently and more severely than their non-Black peers. During in-school and out-of-school suspension, children have little to no access to educational materials and often spend time idle. This time out of class stigmatizes children and keeps them from being up-to-date on lessons.

Unlike Cruz, who prior to becoming an active shooter was able to move through life almost without a criminal record,

Advanced Via Individual Determination (AVID) and African-American Male Initiative (AAMI) are attempts to provide students of color with culturally competent education options.

The School-to-Prison Pipeline

In Florida, the Preventing Recidivism through Opportunities, Mentoring, Interventions, Supports & Education (PROMISE) program was designed to interrupt the school-to-prison pipeline and curb the overrepresentation of minority youth being more severely punished in school, saying its lax discipline structure prevents law enforcement from stepping in soon enough.[20]

This shows how education—by way of institutional racism—leads to greater imprisonment of youths of color. "Zero-tolerance" discipline policies, which are most often used in communities of color, lead to higher rates of punishment of Black and Brown children and thrust them into the criminal justice system early in life. This is called the school-to-prison pipeline—the pathway children of color follow when being punished for minor behaviors that quickly lead to permanent consequences within the legal system.

Turk will forever have a theft charge on his record and is now one step further along the school-to-prison pipeline that exists for Black and Brown youth.

Access to Mentors and Resources

Even one teacher of color can have a significant impact on the education of students of color. It shows that someone like them was able to rise above the challenges they faced and do something impactful. But the teacher workforce is overwhelmingly white.[21] And those teachers often carry biases and negative attitudes that students pick up on, especially in important areas like STEM.[22] Without exposure to diverse teachers, students of color are left to study the same whitewashed curriculum that hardly reflects them, or does so negatively.

Teachers are also the gatekeepers to college readiness for many students, but children of color are less likely to be recommended for talented and gifted programs or assigned to advanced courses.[23] Without teachers who understand their culture and struggles, students of color might not believe they will do well in school at all—let alone attend college.[24]

Past discrimination has left youth of color less likely to have a parent or role model to walk them through the process of college applications, financial aid, and all the other things you must know to get into college. Without mentors to fill the gap, students might miss out on the skills that help them with important foundations in reading and math for college readiness. Without a college degree, it's possible but not likely that you will be able to get a decent job. We're learning that the differences in the quality of education children of color receive have affected how many of them get to go to college.

The American education system ostracizes children of color, and it has unfortunately become a fundamental pillar of institutional racism in this country negatively affecting young peoples' lives and futures.

CHAPTER 3

The Media

In 2018, the US government was serious about holding pharmaceutical companies responsible for producing drugs with addictive qualities. The opioid epidemic led to an estimated 115 American deaths a day.[1] Nationally, individuals on all ends of the political spectrum were pushing to get resources like therapy and medical treatment for those affected. Media coverage showed family members grieving and soliciting great sympathy for those who were victims to addiction.

This isn't the first time the United States faced a wide-scale drug problem. Instead of sympathy or stories on the power of addiction, 30 years ago there was a war on drugs that criminalized Black America.[2] Unlike our current commitment to programs and assistive legislation, there were laws passed to arrest crack addicts with no regard for their families and in the process creating life-long stigma. Instead of compassion, Black homes suspected as crack houses underwent armed raids. Individuals addicted to crack cocaine were portrayed as scum on an otherwise beautiful society.

Similarly, crimes committed by Muslims get 449 percent more coverage and are almost always linked to a larger set of conspiracies like terrorism.[3] On the other hand, a white terrorist—like Stephen Paddock, who killed fifty and injured hundreds in Las Vegas—

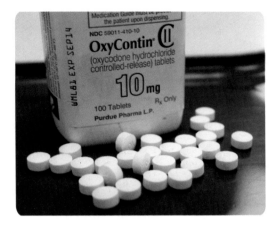

Opioids have taken quite the toll on the United States in the last decade.

is viewed as a lone wolf, and their terrorism is labeled mental illness instead of a religious or racial pathology.[4]

There is nothing new about the media showing Black and Brown folks as inherently criminal. Through the years, the way media channels have shown people of color, especially Black and Muslim people, has fueled harmful stereotypes and caused teachers, employment agencies, and law enforcement to see them as threats and shape their experiences in education, hiring, and the criminal justice system.

Playing a Role

Historically, newspapers and television shows have adjusted stories for increasing viewership. If you want evidence of the ways this adjustment makes things harder for people color, watch the news and pay attention to phrasing.

Take the recent instances of domestic terrorism in the United States. When the person is white, they are typically referred to as a "lone wolf"—someone who is acting alone or out of mental illness. However, when people of color—particularly those of Middle Eastern-appearing descent—are suspected of a crime, they are automatically linked to a wide range of organized terrorism and religious fundamentalism. The crimes of white people are not framed as a pathology (a problem in themselves) of their race or religion. The crimes of people of color are.

We saw this in action in 2005, when New Orleans was almost entirely submerged after Hurricane Katrina.[5] People began looking for food, as anyone would if power and

Hurricane Katrina led to one of the biggest number of housing displacements in American history. Thousands of victims were temporarily housed in the Astrodome, located in Houston, Texas.

resources were limited. But the media portrayal was vastly different. Black individuals were often referred to as looters, a term that points to criminal activity. White individuals doing the same were given more neutral descriptions like "attempting to provide during chaos."[6]

A Community in Distress

One of the most outrageous instances of the media shaping public opinion is the way unarmed Black and Brown individuals—even children—are put "on trial" instead of the officers who killed them. When innocent adults and children of color are killed by the police, the media finds "thug-like" images from their social media and uses language that excuses and even justifies their murder. On the other hand, the media uses the class, yearbook, or family photos for white criminals to show their "civility."

Michael Brown was a Black man accused of stealing candy and cigarettes, which led to his murder by a policeman.[7] Compare this to Ethan Couch, a white man who drove his truck into a crowd and killed four people while drunk driving. Not only was he arrested alive, he made the argument that his wealthy upbringing meant he didn't understand right from wrong. He has since been freed from jail.

As instances of police brutality continue to rise, more communities of color, like Ferguson, are expressing their discontent—often in the form of mass protesting.[8] Instead of showing the decades of negative police community interaction, the media disregards their protest by calling their behavior a riot or making dismissive statements about how

When Michael Brown was killed by police in 2014, the Black community was outraged. National protests and conversations about police brutality occurred, and most are still happening today.

The #SayHerName Campaign Highlights Women of Color

Black and Brown women/girls, like Aiyana Jones—a seven-year-old Black girl who was killed in Detroit during a police raid—are often overlooked in the police brutality discussion. The #SayHerName campaign exists to bring more attention to the Black women who were victims of police brutality and anti-Black violence. As Black and Brown youth are gunned down due to minor suspicion, there have been dozens of white active shooters who made headlines. They have overwhelmingly been arrested alive.

they are destroying their own neighborhoods. Some outlets go as far as calling Ferguson protestors "animals" and other dehumanizing names.[9]

We see similar behavior—fires, property damage, and violence—from white sports fans after their teams win or lose football games. These incidents are framed as all in good fun when the perpetrators are white, but as thuggish when discussing communities like Ferguson that are outraged over life-and-death matters.

Who Belongs Here and Who Doesn't?

The media shapes our national view of who belongs versus who is an "other" in our society. The images we see on a daily basis are the reasons "Black" comes to mind when people talk about crime, Latinxs come to mind when people discuss immigration, and Natives are imagined as alcoholics in a modern context.

White people have the freedom to exist outside of these harmful stereotypes and often get to occupy space that wasn't made for them. An example of this is movies that feature main characters of color who are then cast as white people. When you are free from stereotypical association, you have the freedom to act out someone else's culture however you want.

Asians are rarely portrayed in leading roles in American film or TV. When they make an appearance, it's often a racial stereotype depending on their group. Blacks and Latinxs are often shown in roles that involve violence and gang activity, and Natives are overrepresented in roles that show them as

Media depictions often show Hispanic Americans as drug lords and criminals. These stereotypes shape our conversation on immigration policies and resources for the Latinx community—particularly those who are undocumented.

addicts. While these experiences might represent a narrow subset of what these populations have gone through, they should not be used as the public image of a group of people.

The media plays the number-one role in shaping public opinion, often because many white people do not have diverse friendship circles. The term "token Black friend" refers to how, for many white people, having one Black friend who has expressed a certain mindset or set of life experiences provides them enough information to make conclusions on the thoughts and feelings of all Black people.

Because some white people don't have meaningful relationships with people of color, they take the images they see on the screen and don't have the opportunity to correct these stereotypes. This is harmful and relates to institutional racism because white people in positions of power, like lawmakers and police officers, often make false assumptions about people of color based on what they have seen in the media. We see this in the way white police officers often kill unarmed Black men because they feel their lives were threatened, but armed white suspects are often taken alive. The media has reinforced the idea that Black men are threats.

Fueling Separation

Lately, the media's influence on politics and race relations has been huge. Our nation is currently determining the lasting effect that Russian hackers had on our 2016 presidential election results.[10] One of their most obvious methods was to make racially charged ads and take advantage of America's conflict-filled climate.

The language used by Russian hackers was similar to the harmful language that encourages violence and attacks against Black and Brown folks that we have heard from Donald Trump. The hackers understood that the key to controlling American politics was mentioning the topics we fight over daily, like race, immigration, and terrorism.

False statistics by right-wing media outlets have been used to fuel the new generation of white supremacy referred to as "the alt-right."[11] Because these groups are mostly made up of white men, they are discussed in reasonable

Richard Spencer is one of many who belong to the alt-right, a group of white supremacists that uses hateful rhetorical and false claims to encourage white fear.

terms for their intellectual and well-dressed presentation instead of getting the terrorist label and societal exclusion they deserve.[12]

The media has spun white supremacists into benign-sounding "alt-right," and yet at the same time presents people of color, especially Black men and women, as criminals from birth, creating unjustified fear and distrust from the nation at large. For many, particularly in the cases of police brutality, that fear has cost many people of color their lives. This kind of media bias is a perfect example of institutional racism at work in our society.

CHAPTER 4

The Criminal Justice System

As twelve-year old Tamir Rice played with a toy gun near Cudell Recreation Center, less than 100 yards from his Ohio home, he had no idea it would be his last half hour of life.[1] At 3:22, 911 dispatch received a call from a man calmly reporting someone who was "probably juvenile" pointing a gun at people, but that it was probably fake. This phone call and the dispatcher's failure to relay information that the gun was likely fake lead to the death of Tamir Rice.

When Tamir Rice was killed, the Black community wept harder than they had for any similar tragedy in the last decade. The murder of unarmed Black men and women was nothing new, but the community never expected the personification of racial profiling to fall on the shoulders of a child that young. However, in the eyes of law enforcement, minority children are seen as adults.[2]

That shock was shared by the Latinx community after fourteen-year-old Jesse Romero was killed in 2016. And again, by the Native community with fourteen-year-old Jason Pero in late 2017.

Compare the innocent children above to fifty-seven-year-old Robert L. Dear, who opened fire inside of a Planned Parenthood in late 2015.[3] He killed three, including a police officer, and injured nine others, yet he was captured alive. Similarly, Dylann Roof, Nikolas Cruz, and even Eliza Wasni, who killed her Uber driver with a stolen machete, were all white and apprehended alive, despite being obvious threats.[4,5,6]

When twelve-year-old Tamir Rice was murdered by police in November of 2014, the nation was outraged. Children of color are at risk regardless of age.

What is Police Brutality?

Police brutality is the unnecessary pushing, hitting, or killing of citizens. Though this is an issue that affects people of all ethnicities, victims of police brutality are overwhelmingly people of color. Some believe that because more white people are killed by the police annually that white people are most frequently targeted. This isn't true. White people make up the largest percentage of the population, so it makes sense for them to have higher numbers than people of color. However, probability shows that Black and Brown people are more likely to experience police brutality due to profiling.

While it would be nice to think of the above scenarios as isolated incidents, they are the most painful examples of why communities of color have such strained relationships with law enforcement and the criminal justice system at large and perfect examples of institutionalized racism in action.

From an early age, children of color must be prepared to live in a world where their race robs them of the "innocent until proven guilty" concept our justice system was founded upon.[7] Minority individuals have been at odds with the criminal justice system for centuries and continue to be today.

What Is a Crime? Who Is a Criminal?

Through the years, what is considered a crime and who is a criminal have changed repeatedly. While the way the law is enforced has shifted, it continuously has an unfair effect on men and women of color.

Think about Harriet Tubman who, despite being an American hero for her efforts to free slaves, was a wanted criminal in her time. Centuries later, Rosa Parks showed parallels to Tubman—a Black woman who broke the law but ultimately desired equality. History has a way of overlooking the truth that nearly all our favorite Black history figures were considered criminals in their day. This is because so many of the laws and institutions in America were developed with racism and discrimination against people of color in mind.

The Indian Removal Act forced Native Americans off their land and designated them criminals if they returned.[8]

Rosa Parks, famous for the Montgomery bus boycotts, was one of many key civil rights figures.

Thanks to the Dakota Access Pipeline, Natives can be designated as criminals for protesting its placement in land that is owned by them and inherently connected to them through history and ancestry.

Today, Hispanic/Latinx crossing the border to seek the "American Dream" are labeled criminals. The well-known S.B. 1070, or Arizona Anti-Immigration Law, allows officers to question those who "look like undocumented citizens."[9] This kind of racial profiling is something Black Americans are all too familiar with.

You can see throughout American history that people of color were often criminals by default, even when that crime was wanting equality or simply existing.[10]

Signs of Institutional Racism in the Criminal Justice System

The problem of institutional racism starts long before we heard stories of Black and Brown children being murdered by police. We see institutional racism in the unequal surveillance, harsher sentencing, and higher rates of imprisonment experienced by people of color.

Increased Surveillance

In 2013, Oscar-winning actor Forest Whitaker was accused of shoplifting after a morning attempt to purchase yogurt. This situation wasn't nearly as traumatizing as the experience of American scholar and Harvard professor Henry Louis Gates Jr., who was arrested after being accused of breaking into his own home.[11] These high-profile Black men show what many people of color understand: no amount of money can buy a way out of racial profiling.

In the United States, 24 percent of Black Americans feel discriminated against while shopping.[12] Speak to any person of color, and they will probably tell you they have been followed around a store or watched a little too closely while shopping. The signs that dominant forces in society believe people of color, particularly Black people, are more likely to commit crimes are everywhere. There is no reason to believe white people are less likely to commit crimes than minorities, but there is evidence people of color will be more severely punished for them.[13]

In 2013, efforts were made to change the way law enforcement interacted with people of color. Federal judge Shira Scheindlin ruled that the New York Police Department (NYPD) was not allowed to use stop-and-frisk tactics.[14,15] Stop-and-frisk was created out of a belief that you could prevent "suspicious looking" individuals from committing crimes by stopping them on the streets and checking to see if they had weapons or drugs.

The process wouldn't have been as problematic if it didn't target people of color at drastically higher rates than white

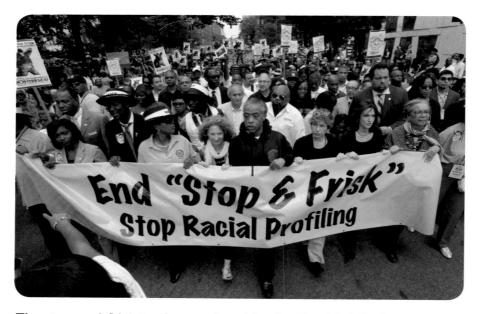

The stop-and-frisk tactics employed by the New York Police Department were controversial from the start. Thankfully, Judge Shira Scheindlin rendered the law unconstitutional 2013.

people. But as noted earlier, the expectation that people of color were more likely to commit crimes motivated this tactic. The results, however, suggested differently: Not only were people of color more likely to be stopped, but they were also less likely to possess drugs or weapons than white people. The findings spoke for themselves, and stop-and-frisk was ultimately ruled a violation of constitutional rights.[16]

Challenging the practices of one police department motivated researchers to investigate the way law enforcement interacts with people of color. Sadly, stop-and-frisk is just one organized example of racial profiling in the criminal justice system that promotes institutional racism.

Harsher Sentencing

In her book *Weapons of Math Destruction*, mathematician Cathy O'Neil makes the claim that if you live in an area with increased police presence, you're more likely to be punished for a crime—not because you were more likely to commit one, but because you were more likely to get caught. After you are accused of criminal activity, you become a criminal defendant. The Fourth, Fifth, Sixth, and Eighth Amendments of the U.S. Constitution provide information on your rights from the trial forward.[17] You're supposed to be read these rights when you are arrested.[18] However, because of institutional racism, these rights as Americans don't always benefit people of color.

Highlights

Black Americans are **two times more likely** to have their car searched.[19] Black Americans are **nearly five times more likely** to go to prison for drug possession as white people, even though drug use rates are about the same.[20] In some states, like Louisiana, Black Americans were up to **twenty-three times more likely** to be sentenced to life without parole.[21] Innocent Black Americans are **seven times more likely** to be convicted of murder than innocent white Americans.[22] Black Americans are **twice as likely** to be excluded from jury duty due to race.[23] Black Americans have **10 percent longer sentences** for the same crimes as white people.[24] It varies by state, but in places like Dallas, Texas, Black Americans are **55 percent more likely** to have probation revoked.[25]

Thanks to discrimination, Black men are imprisoned at rates that are many times the national average.

Rates of Imprisonment

Putting all this into context, it's not surprising that people of color are jailed at much higher rates. According to the Sentencing Project, an organization that helps us understand and fight prison injustice:

> "One in 17 black men aged 30–34 was in prison in 2015, as were 1 in 42 Hispanic males and 1 in 91 white males in the same age group. Also, Black women were double as likely to be in prison as white women and Hispanic women were 1.2 times as likely."[26]

There are so many Black men in jail that more than 1.5 million are considered missing by their families.[27]

These examples of institutional racism aren't just an issue for minority adults. Youth of color are more likely to experience harsher punishments as well. In 2014 and 2017, research confirmed what Black parents already knew: Black children are seen as less innocent than white children.[28,29]

Here are some statistics that show this for youth of color:

- Black youth make up 16 percent of the population, but 44 percent of youths held in juvenile facilities. Black youth are 28 percent of juvenile arrests, 37 percent of the youths in juvenile jails, and 58 percent of the youths sent to adult prison.[30]

- Black youth are five times more likely than white youth to be detained or committed.[31]

- Latinx youth are 65 percent more likely to be detained or committed than their white peers.[32]

- Native youth are three times as likely to be incarcerated.[33]

The 13th Amendment and Disenfranchisement

The 13th Amendment is remembered as the end of slavery. But its phrasing, particularly the following, "Neither slavery nor involuntary servitude, except as a punishment for crime," has long-term consequences for the Black community. One of the earliest instances of this was convict leasing—a system that took prisoners, whom were overwhelmingly Black, and used them for free labor throughout the South. Conditions have slightly improved for prisons now, but prisoners still perform unpaid labor.

The longest-lasting effects of the criminal justice system come after prison. Examples include losing the right to vote, near impossibility of getting a good-paying job, loss of parental rights, and being ineligible for federal and state assistance. Some places, like Florida, are working to restore the right to vote for ex-convicts, but for Black and Brown people who spend time in prison, their lives will never be the same.

Advocates for improving the criminal justice system, like the Sentencing Project, don't think people of color should not be punished for the crimes they commit. Instead, they believe people of color should be treated the same as whites, especially when they have committed the same or similar crime.

CHAPTER 5

Wealth

Money and finances affect every area of our lives. In America, 41 percent of children are considered low-income. But when we look at the numbers by race, Black children experienced the highest rates of low-income and deep poverty (61 percent and 17 percent), followed closely by Native children (60 percent and 18 percent), and Latinx children (59 percent and 11 percent), compared to White (28 percent and 5 percent) and Asian (28 percent and 4 percent) children.[1] Black, Native, and Latino children are nearly three times as likely to live in poverty.

American society places a great emphasis on the importance of credit, assets, and wealth. But there are two factors that affect the amount of money someone has access to: jobs available and money prior generations were able to hold on to. Why some families have more money than others goes along with the way race and institutional discrimination have led to unequal wealth distribution. There are many ways America's racist past has led to current wealth gaps. Here's one that's easiest to see today: hiring discrimination.

One of the main drivers of the wealth gap in the United States is the history of job discrimination. Of course, this is made worse through wage gaps and refusing to promote qualified candidates.

Unpacking the "Bootstrap Myth"

The bootstrap myth refers to the false belief that persistence and hard work are enough to get you out of financial struggle. This myth has been used to blame people of color for worse financial outcomes. The truth is whiteness and inheritance have lead to better opportunity and social connections for white people.[2] Unfortunately, no amount of hard work can help people of color avoid the number of obstacles that stand between them and equality. White people have several hundred years of a head start from profiting off of others.

Can't Buy a Good Job

For Black Americans, finding a good job is challenging. Although the national unemployment rate was 3.9 percent in the fourth quarter of 2017, the unemployment rate for

Black Americans was 7 percent. Compare that to 2.4 percent for Asians, 3.4 percent for whites, and 4.7 percent for Latinxs, and it's clear that Black Americans are consistently almost double most groups.[3] An untrained eye would interpret the rates as a matter of motivation and overlook look systemic causes. Thankfully, researchers are working to provide a more holistic perspective.

A recent study done by Northwestern University found that despite affirmative action programs, job prospects have shown almost no reduction in job discrimination in 25 years.[4] Latinxs saw a very slight reduction, but Black Americans are facing the same struggles from decades ago. During the study, they found that white Americans got roughly 36 percent more callbacks than equally qualified Black Americans and about 24 percent more than their Latinx counterparts.

If you are wondering how résumés and job calls can still encourage racial discrimination, look no further than a name.

What's in a Name?

One of the most common ways individuals of color are discriminated against in the job market is by their names. While Black Americans with stereotypical names are more likely to be passed over for a job despite qualifications, they aren't the only ones.

In 2016, Asian American Tiffany Trieu applied for a job as a graphic designer.[5] The president of the company responded with a letter saying they had already hired enough foreign nationals and needed to hire an American to avoid being unfair. The kicker? Trieu was born in the United States and is

Women of color are discriminated against on multiple grounds. This makes it very difficult to get hired for high-paying jobs and be promoted for those who are hired.

an American citizen. Though under-discussed, this experience isn't a rarity for job seekers of Asian descent. South Asians (individuals from Afghanistan, Bangladesh, Bhutan, India, Maldives, Pakistan, Nepal, and Sri Lanka) along with individuals with Muslim-sounding names are often targets,

What's in a Name?

Tiffany Trieu's experience is common for people of color. Interviewers and job screening tools often try to guess a candidate's ethnicity by their name. Historically, higher-paying jobs didn't hire people of color due to individual racism. Now, institutional racism is excluding worthy job candidates based off name, and indirectly, race. It goes without saying that the name or race of a potential job candidate shouldn't be a factor in deciding who is qualified to do a job.

thanks to false narratives on terrorism and other hate-based sentiments that can affect their job prospects.[6]

Differences in Income

When people of color are hired, they are often paid less or find themselves stuck in lower-level positions.

The wage gap is a key component of the differences in household incomes. The most commonly discussed figures are that white women make 79 cents for every white man's dollar, Black women 66 cents, and Latinx women 59 cents.[7] Critics argue that certain career choices, life decisions, and non-measurable factors lead to these differences. But the bottom line is less money is being brought into households of color.

The median income for Black Americans is $36,898, as compared to the $62,950 median income for white families and $45,148 for a Latinx household.[8] Education, criminal justice experiences, and media representation work together to affect job opportunities for people of color. Unfortunately, even when adjusting for those setbacks, people of color and particularly Black people have worse experiences than their white counterparts. With no high school diploma, the median income by race is $30,000 for white people, $22,000 for Latinxs, and $20,500 for Blacks.[9] With a college degree, that figure increases but hardly evens out. White Americans with a bachelor's degree make $50,000, Black Americans make a little less than $45,000, and Latinxs bring in a little less than $46,000. It's important to note that the median household income for Asians is misleading. The term "Asian" lumps tens

Legally, we should all be protected from job-related mistreatment regardless of sex, race, orientation, and gender. These things all have a substantial effect on our opportunities for success.

of varying cultures together and overlooks the financial struggles of certain Asian subgroups.

The Racial Wealth Gap

Many white Americans believe that an increase of people of color in high-paying job fields means equal opportunities to make money.[10] While wages may be improving, wealth—what people of color have to pass on to the next generation— shows that things are still bad.

When examined in 2016, the median wealth of Black ($17,600) and Latinx ($20,700) families painted a sad picture.[11] That picture was even sadder when compared against the $171,000 median for white families. Wages have had an effect on the wealth gap, but the biggest cause is that Black Americans and other people of color got a late start in gaining and growing that wealth.

Limited Job Access

While the white American economy had centuries of profit from slavery, Black males were often limited to low-paying field labor. Black women were often limited to caretaking roles and often had limited access to their own children. After years of domestic labor, Jim Crow laws—state and local rules that made it legal to discriminate based on race—prevented

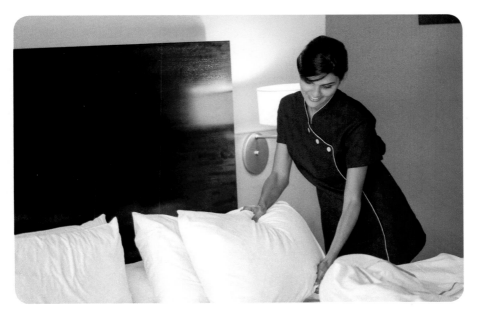

Latinx women are overrepresented in jobs like waitressing and housekeeping. Unfortunately, even when they find employment in other realms, they are often mistaken for "the help."

Black Americans from equal public facility use, let alone high-paying jobs.[12] Contemporarily, Hispanic/Latinx individuals are in roles similar to that of Black Americans decades ago, like housekeeping and back-of-kitchen work.

Housing Discrimination

Owning a house means having wealth to pass down to future generations. Similarly, wills and life insurance pass money down the family tree. Black Americans and other people of color were often excluded from many of the government-sponsored programs that helped white America acquire and transfer wealth.

- Limited housing access: Places like Levittown explicitly prohibited non-whites from moving into the housing development. At one point, the lease agreement read, "The tenant agrees not to permit the premises to be sued or occupied by any person other than members of the Caucasian race."[13]

- Redlining: When the New Deal—government assistance programs created with the goal of helping Americans after the Great Depression—created loans to help Americans finance housing, Black Americans were excluded and designated to "red" or bad neighborhoods, and whites were designated "green" or good neighborhoods.[14,15] Green areas had easy access to home loans; red, not so much. For decades, Black and Native veterans were excluded from being able to use Veterans Affairs housing loans that white veterans could use to buy homes with minimal to zero interest.

From its start, the housing market worked hard to keep neighborhoods and schools as white as possible. As a result, many neighborhoods and schools are still segregated.

- Increased financial struggles: Black Americans have higher rates of foreclosure as a result of being given worse loan terms and having generally lower wages. The consequences of falling behind on a mortgage can lead to lifelong issues for people of color. Unlike their white counterparts, Black Americans are encouraged to pursue Chapter 13 (bankruptcy), which requires making payments on debt and can lead to money being taken out of their paychecks, as opposed to Chapter 7, which wipes out debt and protects what you have.[16]

Housing discrimination was a problem in the past and continues to be one now.

From the 1930s to the late 1960s, home ownership was a benefit for white people almost exclusively. These neighborhoods attracted new businesses, ultimately increasing property values. People of color were often excluded from these areas, and were limited to poor and underserved neighborhoods.

ProPublica found that Blacks and Latinxs experience at least 4 million cases of illegal housing discrimination per year. By being charged higher interest rates and mortgage terms than white Americans regardless of credit scores, Black and Latinx individuals are still systemically limited from the biggest wealth generator today: home ownership.[17]

CHAPTER 6

Health

Diabetes, a condition when your body struggles to process food into energy, is a common health condition in Native, Black, and Latinx communities. Type 2 and gestational diabetes are related to the foods you eat as well as how often you exercise, and both are affected by institutional racism. For example, people of color are more likely to live in food deserts, or areas that lack affordable fruits, vegetables, whole grains, low-fat milk, and other fresh foods that you need to be healthy. Food deserts are filled with cheap fast-food restaurants but have few grocery stores. More than half of all areas with incomes of less than $25,000 meet the definition of food desert.[1]

If you are a struggling family or a single parent working several jobs, it's hard to find time to make dinner, let alone research each ingredient in the food you eat. Similarly, gym memberships are expensive, and many people of color don't participate in easier exercises like walking because often there isn't a safe place to walk in the neighborhood.

As mainstream grocery stores overlook the needs of rural areas and communities of color, Daily Table is a nonprofit that aims to increase access to healthy food to inner city communities.

When we talk about health outcomes, we typically focus on an individual's behaviors. These are important. However, focusing on individual actions might cause us to miss out on the way institutional racism has led to disparities in the health care system.

A Not-So-Distant Past

The way people of color were treated since slavery and the Native American genocide greatly affect their views on the health care industry today. The continued mistreatment, medical horror stories passed down through families, and new research on differences in care make these communities feel they cannot trust the health care system. It's equally important to know that segregation and limiting access to health care on Native reservations have been deadly to marginalized groups.

Experimentation on Slaves

Slaves were property not people, and there are many cases where slaves were used for human experiments.[2] One of the most infamous tales of experimentation follows Lucy, Betsey, and Anarcha, slave women whom James Marion Sims practiced on to perfect the techniques that resulted in him being named the father of modern gynecology.[3] Sims performed more than 30 surgeries, without anesthesia, on Anarcha alone.

Eugenics Movement

In an attempt to rid American society of "undesirables," many states allowed the sterilization— altering reproductive organs so that the person cannot have children—of an estimated 60,000 individuals, many of whom were Black, Native, and Latinx. Between 1973 and 1976, 3,046 Native women had been sterilized by the Indian Health Service without their consent.[4,5,6]

James Marion Sims is treated as the father of modern gynecology.

Tuskegee Experiments

In 1932, the Public Health Service and Tuskegee Institute worked together to start the "Tuskegee Study of Untreated Syphilis in the Negro Male." They lured participants in by promising access to health care and telling them they had "bad blood," but never informing them of the purpose of the study. For more than forty years, the researchers avoided treating 399 of the 600 men who had syphilis despite having access to a cure because they wanted to watch the course of the disease.[7]

Financial Barriers

Blacks and Latinxs are often limited to subpar medical care because quality service follows money. The Indian Health Service exists for Natives' health care, but the per patient spending of $2,849 is nothing compared with national rates of $7,717 per person.[8] Additionally, government programs

Dismantling Systemic Racism in Health Care

Dr. Rupa K. Marya is at the frontlines of educating individuals about racism in health care. In addition to being Associate Professor of Medicine at the University of California, San Francisco, she is a human rights activist who was involved in the Standing Rock protests and is working to open a free, integrative health care clinic on the reservation. She was also involved in starting the Do No Harm Coalition in May 2016 to end police violence and change policing practices in San Francisco and elsewhere.

spend more money on conditions that affect white citizens than people of color. For example, see state-sponsored rehab for opioid abusers and prison sentences for crack users.

Limited access to culturally competent mental health professionals makes dealing with these issues even harder. Black and Native individuals have some of the highest rates of mental health issues but hardly any professionals available in their communities trained to treat them.[9] All of these affect the quality of care received by people of color. But racism is most easily seen in the differences in health outcomes and treatment they face.

Youth and adults of color often lack the resources to find quality mental health care. Much of this is due to the fact that few mental health professionals are of color or culturally comeptent. Stigma also makes dealing with these stressors difficult for many people.

The Consequences of Cultural Insensitivity

Race matters when receiving health care services. When seeking treatment, people of color often face stereotyping, worse bedside manner, and higher rates of medical mishaps.[10] But the worst experiences are when people of color are disregarded completely.

Black women have a maternal mortality rate that is three to four times the national average, and statistics for Native and Latinx women are hardly tracked.[11] Black infants die at a rate higher than any other ethnicity and nearly two times the white infant mortality rate in the United States.[12]

Natives are dying from opioid addiction at some of the highest rates, but are being left out of the conversation almost entirely.[13] Native children have four times as many untreated tooth decay cases as white children. Natives numbering 2.4 million suffer from dental issues due to limited access to dental care.[14] Natives are 552 percent more likely to die from alcoholism than any other group.[15]

Institutional Racism Discourages Assistance and Victim-Blames

Institutionalized racism in the medical industry makes people of color afraid to seek care that they need. When they do seek care, they are often met with negative experiences filled with stereotyping and mistreatment.

Many of the health conditions that plague people of color are a consequence of the environment they are forced to live in. Think of it this way: Less money means an inability to escape your circumstances. Not being able to escape can mean increased exposure to violence (which negatively affects mental health), lower access to healthy foods (many people of color live in food deserts with limited access to fresh foods and grocery stores), and less access to good jobs that help you support yourself. Sometimes, the areas where people of color grow up are just plain toxic. Flint, Michigan, is an area that has been dealing with lead-filled water for years. Exposure to lead has lifelong effects, such as cancer, limited brain development, and death.[16]

Some like to think that lack of education and finances are the only reasons for racial health disparities. But it's worth

The People's Organization for Progress is an example of the many organizations fighting against war, racism, and the mistreatment of marginalized individuals.

noting that the environments that people of color grow up in, paired with chronic exposure to stress, also effects their health outcomes. Research on middle-class and higher-income people of color found that Black people who move to a higher financial class often have worse health outcomes.[17] Black women with PhDs still die from birth-related complications at a rate similar to white women with a high school diploma. The exact reason is unknown, but professionals believe it's the result of continuous exposure to racism, "toxic stress," and assumptions by medical professionals. An example of this was in 2018, when tennis superstar Serena Williams wasn't taken seriously after she described symptoms of a pulmonary embolism, which is when a blood clot makes its way to the lungs, after giving birth. For many people of color, moving to a "better" neighborhood often comes with more stress, more encounters with racism, and heightened feelings of social pressure.

The American Psychological Association discusses the importance of looking at cultural factors while providing physical and mental health care, something that is lacking in most health care services.[18] The extreme mistreatment people of color experienced set the foundation for institutional racism in the health care industry. To do more to close gaps in health care, people at every level of health care need to evaluate how stereotypes, past medical mistreatment, and cultural assumptions have indirectly caused worse care for people of color. By making sure medical professionals are trained in cultural differences, we can improve the medical system one person at a time.

CHAPTER 7

Current Resistance Movements

With so much bad news, it's easy to feel overwhelmed by the state of things. Thankfully, there is comfort in remembering that pioneers for social change and all the civil rights greats have seen and overcome worse.

Resources for Resistance

Any time discrimination arises, there are organizations that fight back for justice. Here are a few organizations that work to improve the social conditions for people of color:

The American Civil Liberties Union (ACLU) works within the legal system to ensure equal access to constitutional rights, like freedom of speech, right to privacy, and freedom of religion.

The National Association for the Advancement of Colored People (NAACP) is an organization that works to get rid of racism and racial prejudice while fighting for equality of rights for all people.

It's difficult to think about organizations that fight for social change without the NAACP coming to mind. Since 1909, it has been at the forefront of anti-discrimination efforts.

#NotInvisible is a movement aimed to increase awareness for Native women and girls who are victims of sexual assault, along with raising awareness around Missing and Murdered Indigenous Women and Girls (MMIWG).

#SayHerName is another social media campaign to increase the visibility of Black women victims of police violence.

The American Indian Movement (AIM) is a historic organization that aims to increase the quality of life of Natives in a variety of areas.

Black Lives Matter (BLM) is an intersectional movement that aims to improve the lives of all Black Americans, including sexual and gender minorities who have been marginalized by previous Black empowerment movements.

Culturally responsive curriculums prioritizing teaching provide materials that engage diverse groups of students and have been proven to lead to better outcomes for students of color.

European Dissent is an organization of white anti-racist organizers committed to social change.

Restorative Justice is a push to shift school disciplinary actions from isolation-based to increased mentorship and student redirection.

Individuals from all over came to show their support for the Lakota Sioux tribe despite resistance from local authorities.

In recent years, South Asian Americans have begun to mobilize and engage in activism related to community affairs.

South Asian Americans Leading Together (SAALT) is a nonprofit that centers the needs of South Asian students and advocates for policy that improves conditions for South Asians, including gender justice, resisting 9/11 backlash, and increasing civic engagement within the community.

TransWomen of Color Collective is a national organizing collective led by trans women of color to uplift the narratives, leadership, and lived experiences of trans and gender non-conforming people of color.

The Sentencing Project is a nonprofit that works for a fair and effective U.S. criminal justice system by promoting reforms in sentencing policy, addressing unjust racial disparities and practices, and advocating for alternatives to incarceration.

Moving Forward

Institutional racism affects every area of life for people of color. It limits their access to a quality education, makes it harder to find jobs to provide for their families, and even affects the quality of care they receive from the medical system. However, it's important to remember that organizations that are successful in making longstanding change are made up of people who are determined to push our nation closer toward equality.

The importance of voting in local elections cannot be overstated.
Your vote is your voice. Never allow anyone to take your voice away.

We all have a shared responsibility to join that fight by using our privileges to make life better for those who are disadvantaged. Getting involved in a resistance organization or campaign is just one way to help dismantle systems of institutional racism in America. One of the most direct ways to effect change nationally and locally is by exercising your right to vote. Voting locally is especially important. That way, when you hear of policies that have negative effects on marginalized people, you can remind your community to move forward not backward. The students who attended Marjory Stoneman Douglas High School in Parkland, Florida, have made reminding legislators that if they do not represent their interests, they will vote them out when they turn 18 a considerable part of their message. You have the power to do the same with your vote.

Chapter Notes

Chapter 1
What Is Institutional Racism?

1. "The Civil Rights Act of 1964," History.com, accessed March 2018, https://www.history.com/topics/black-history/civil-rights-act
2. "On Views of Race and Inequality, Blacks and Whites Are Worlds Apart," Pew Research Center, June 27, 2016, http://www.pewsocialtrends.org/2016/06/27/on-views-of-race-and-inequality-blacks-and-whites-are-worlds-apart
3. "Serena Williams Fires Back at Ilie Nastase Over 'Racist' Comment," *New York Times*, April 25, 2017, https://www.nytimes.com/2017/04/25/sports/tennis/serena-williams-ilie-nastase.html

Chapter 2
Education

1. "Update: African-American girl won't face expulsion over 'natural hair,'" *News 6*, November 27, 2013, https://www.clickorlando.com/news/update-african-american-girl-wont-face-expulsion-over-natural-hair
2. Rebecca Klein, "Tiana Parker, 7, Switches Schools After Being Forbidden from Wearing Dreads," *Huffington Post*, September 5, 2013, https://www.huffingtonpost.com/2013/09/05/tiana-parker-dreads_n_3873868.html
3. "Parent/Student Handbook 2007–2008," Deborah Brown Community School, accessed March 2018, http://www.dbcschool.org/admin/files/P46e588228bde4/SY%2007%20Parent%20Student%20Handbook.pdf
4. Rebecca Klein, "Native American Child Reportedly Sent Home from Kindergarten Because of Long Hair," *Huffington Post*, September 2, 2014, https://www.huffingtonpost.com/2014/09/02/malachi-wilson-hair_n_5753982.html
5. Christina Sterbenz, "An 8th grader had to teach a math class for a month because Detroit schools were so understaffed, lawsuit alleges," *Business Insider*, September 16, 2016, www.businessinsider.com/michigan-public-schools-lawsuit-2016-9
6. Mark Binelli, "Michigan Gambled on Charter Schools. Its Children Lost." *New York Times*, September 5, 2017, https://www.nytimes.com/2017/09/05/magazine/michigan-gambled-on-charter-schools-its-children-lost.html?mtrref=www.google.com
7. "Researchers: Detroit, Cleveland, Buffalo, Cincinnati, Newark Lead Nation in Child Poverty," National Center for Children in Poverty (NCCP), accessed March 2018, www.nccp.org/media/releases/release_153.html
8. "More Than 40% of Low-Income Schools Don't Get a Fair Share of State and Local Funds, Department of Education Research Finds," U.S. Department of Education, November 30, 2011, https://www.ed.gov/news/press-releases/more-40-low-income-schools-dont-get-fair-share-state-and-local-funds-department-
9. Carl Boisrond, "If Your Teacher Looks Like You, You May Do Better in School," National Public Radio (NPR), September 29, 2017, https://www.npr.org/sections/ed/2017/09/29/552929074/if-your-teacher-looks-likes-you-you-may-do-better-in-school

10. Meredith Broussard, "Why Poor Schools Can't Win at Standardized Testing," *Atlantic*, July 15, 2014, https://www.theatlantic.com/education/archive/2014/07/why-poor-schools-cant-win-at-standardized-testing/374287

11. "Status and Trends in the Education of Racial and Ethnic Groups 2016," National Center for Education Statistics (NCES), August 2016, https://nces.ed.gov/pubs2016/2016007.pdf

12. "Don't Call Them Dropouts: Understanding the Experiences of Young People Who Leave High School Before Graduation," American Promise, May 20, 2014, http://www.americaspromise.org/report/dont-call-them-dropouts

13. Scott Jaschik, "Expectations, Race and College Success," *Inside Higher Ed*, October 24, 2017, https://www.insidehighered.com/news/2017/10/24/study-finds-high-school-teachers-have-differing-expectations-black-and-white

14. Dave Collins, "Minority parents sue over racial quotas at magnet schools," *U.S. News*, February 15, 2018, https://www.usnews.com/news/best-states/connecticut/articles/2018-02-15/parents-sue-over-racial-quotas-at-magnet-schools

15. Jess Clark, "Are the Top New Orleans Public Schools Weeding Out Certain Kids?" WWNO, January 30, 2018, http://wwno.org/post/are-top-new-orleans-public-schools-weeding-out-certain-kids

16. Curt Anderson, Brendan Farrington, and Josh Replogle, "Nikolas Cruz Indicted on 17 Counts of Murder for Florida School Shooting," *Time Magazine*, March 7, 2018, http://time.com/5190374/nikolas-cruz-murder-florida-school-shooting

17. "Red flags: The troubled path of accused Parkland shooter Nikolas Cruz," *Washington Post*, March 10, 2018, https://www.washingtonpost.com/graphics/2018/national/timeline-parkland-shooter-nikolas-cruz/?utm_term=.ac092cc2a13a

18. Scott Wise, "Virginia student charged with stealing 'free' milk from school," *CBS 6*, May 23, 2016, wtvr.com/2016/05/23/free-milk-theft

19. "A First Look: 2013–2014 Civil Rights Data Collection," U.S. Department of Education Office for Civil Rights, accessed March 2018, https://www2.ed.gov/about/offices/list/ocr/docs/2013-14-first-look.pdf

20. "PROMISE Program," Diversity, Prevention & Intervention, accessed March 2018, https://www.browardprevention.org/behavior/promise

21. "The State of Racial Diversity in the Educator Workforce," U.S. Department of Education, July 2016, https://www2.ed.gov/rschstat/eval/highered/racial-diversity/state-racial-diversity-workforce.pdf

22. "Teacher Racial Bias Matters More for Students of Color," Steinhardt School of Culture, Education, and Human Development, May 18, 2017, https://steinhardt.nyu.edu/site/ataglance/2017/05/teacher-racial-bias-matters-more-for-students-of-color.html

23. Jason A. Grissom and Christopher Redding, "Discretion and Disproportionality: Explaining the Underrepresentation of High-Achieving Students of Color in Gifted Programs," American Educational Research Association, accessed March 2018, www.aera.net/Newsroom/News-Releases-and-Statements/Does-Student-Race-Affect-Gifted-Assignment/Discretion-and-Disproportionality-Explaining-the-Underrepresentation-of-High-Achieving-Students-of-Color-in-Gifted-Programs

24. Desiree Martinez, "Dear High School Teacher Who Tried to Discourage Me from Applying to UCLA, I'm a BRUIN Now!" *LA Comadre*, August 15, 2017, http://lacomadre.org/2017/08/dear-high-school-teacher-tried-discourage-applying-ucla-im-bruin-now

Chapter 3
The Media

1. "Understanding the Epidemic," Centers for Disease Control and Prevention (CDC), accessed March 2018, https://www.cdc.gov/drugoverdose/epidemic/index.html
2. Michael Shaw, "Photos reveal media's softer tone on opioid crisis," *Columbia Journal Review*, July 26, 2017, https://www.cjr.org/criticism/opioid-crisis-photos.php?link
3. Erin Kearns, Allison Betus, and Anthony Lemieux, "Why Do Some Terrorist Attacks Receive More Media Attention Than Others?" March 5, 2017, https://ssrn.com/abstract=2928138
4. Aja Romano, Libby Nelson, Alex Abad-Santos, and German Lopez, "Las Vegas shooting: what we know so far," *Vox*, October 2, 2017, https://www.vox.com/2017/10/2/16395600/las-vegas-shooting-updates
5. Tania Ralli, "Who's a Looter? In Storm's Aftermath, Pictures Kick Up a Different Kind of Tempest," *New York Times*, September 05, 2005, http://www.nytimes.com/2005/09/05/business/whos-a-looter-in-storms-aftermath-pictures-kick-up-a-different.html?mtrref=undefined&mtrref=www.nytimes.
6. Colleen Shalby, "What's the difference between 'looting' and 'finding'? 12 years after Katrina, Harvey sparks a new debate," *Los Angeles Times*, August 29, 2017, http://www.latimes.com/nation/la-na-harvey-20170829-story.html
7. "PDF: Autopsy report for Michael Brown," *St. Louis Post-Dispatch*, October 21, 2014, www.stltoday.com/online/pdf-autopsy-report-for-michael-brown/pdf_ce018d0c-5998-11e4-b700-001a4bcf6878.html
8. "Q&A What Happened in Ferguson?" *New York Times*, August 13, 2014, https://www.nytimes.com/interactive/2014/08/13/us/ferguson-missouri-town-under-siege-after-police-shooting.html?mtrref=undefined&mtrref=www.nytimes.com&gwh=54D90D4D50407132F78A9CCBC81B99EC&gwt=pay
9. Eric Deggans, "LA Riot Documentaries Show Dehumanizing Black People Enables Abuses in Policing," National Public Radio (NPR), April 23, 2017, https://www.npr.org/2017/04/23/525339900/la-riot-documentaries-show-dehumanizing-black-people-enables-abuses-in-policing
10. Eric Westervelt, "How Russia Weaponized Social Media with 'Social Bots,'" National Public Radio (NPR), November 05, 2017, https://www.npr.org/2017/11/05/562058208/how-russia-weaponized-social-media-with-social-bots
11. Philip Bump, "Donald Trumps retweets false race and murder stats from fictional organization," *Independent*, November 23, 2015, http://www.independent.co.uk/news/world/americas/donald-trumps-retweets-false-race-and-murder-stats-from-fictional-organisation-a6744766.html
12. Cam Wolf, "The New Uniform of White Supremacy," *GQ*, August 17, 2017, https://www.gq.com/story/uniform-of-white-supremacy

Chapter 4

The Criminal Justice System

1. Michael Muskal, "Tamir Rice autopsy: Boy with toy gun was shot once by Cleveland cop," *Los Angeles Times*, December 12 2014, http://www.latimes.com/nation/nationnow/la-na-tamir-rice-autopsy-20141212-story.html
2. "The Essence of Innocence: Consequences of Dehumanizing Black Children," American Psychological Association, accessed March 2018, http://www.apa.org/pubs/journals/releases/psp-a0035663.pdf
3. Julie Turkewitz and Jack Healy, "3 Are Dead in Colorado Springs Shootout at Planned Parenthood Center," *New York Times*, November 28, 2015, https://www.nytimes.com/2015/11/28/us/colorado-planned-parenthood-shooting.html
4. Ray Sanchez and Ed Payne, "Charleston church shooting: Who is Dylann Roof?" CNN, June 16, 2015, https://www.cnn.com/2015/06/19/us/charleston-church-shooting-suspect/index.html
5. Ray Sanchez, "Florida school shooter Nikolas Cruz indicted on 34 counts, including premeditated murder," CNN, March 07, 2018, https://www.cnn.com/2018/03/07/us/nikolas-cruz-indictment/index.html
6. Samantha Schmidt, "Teen accused of killing Uber driver with machete in one hand, knife in the other," *Washington Post*, June, 01, 2017, https://www.washingtonpost.com/news/morning-mix/wp/2017/06/01/teenage-girl-kills-uber-driver-with-machete-in-one-hand-knife-in-the-other/?utm_term=.ba183d24b172
7. "Presumption of Innocence," Legal Information Institute, accessed March 2018, https://www.law.cornell.edu/wex/presumption_of_innocence
8. "Indian Removal Act," Library of Congress, accessed March 2018, https://www.loc.gov/rr/program/bib/ourdocs/Indian.html
9. "Valle del Sol v. Whiting," ACLU, accessed March 2018, https://www.aclu.org/cases/valle-del-sol-v-whiting-et-al?redirect=immigrants-rights/valle-del-sol-v-whiting-et-al
10. "Presumption of Guilt," Equal Justice Initiative, accessed March 2018, https://eji.org/racial-justice/presumption-guilt
11. Abby Goodnough, "Harvard Professor Jailed; Officer Is Accused of Bias," *New York Times*, July 21, 2009, http://www.nytimes.com/2009/07/21/us/21gates.html
12. Frank Newport, "In U.S., 24% of Young Black Men Say Police Dealings Unfair," Gallup, July 16, 2013, http://news.gallup.com/poll/163523/one-four-young-black-men-say-police-dealings-unfair
13. Josh Salman, Emily Le Coz, and Elizabeth Johnson, "Florida's broken sentencing system," *Herald Tribune*, accessed March 2018, http://projects.heraldtribune.com/bias/sentencing
14. "Landmark Decision: Judge Rules NYPD Stop and Frisk Practices Unconstitutional, Racially Discriminatory," Center for Constitutional Rights, August 12, 2013, https://ccrjustice.org/home/press-center/press-releases/landmark-decision-judge-rules-nypd-stop-and-frisk-practices
15. "Stop-and-Frisk Data," New York Civil Liberties Union, accessed March 2018, https://www.nyclu.org/en/stop-and-Frisk-data

16. Aviva Shen, "White People Stopped by New York Police Are More Likely to Have Guns or Drugs Than Minorities," ThinkProgress, May 22, 2013, https://thinkprogress.org/white-people-stopped-by-new-york-police-are-more-likely-to-have-guns-or-drugs-than-minorities-9bf579a2b9b3

17. "The United States Bill of Rights: First 10 Amendments to the Constitution," ACLU, accessed March 2018, https://www.aclu.org/united-states-bill-rights-first-10-amendments-constitution

18. "What Are Your Miranda Rights?" Miranda Warning, accessed March 2018, http://www.mirandawarning.org/whatareyourmirandarights.html

19. E. Pierson, C. Simoiu, J. Overgoor, S. Corbett-Davies, V. Ramachandran, C. Phillips, and S. Goel. (2017) "A large-scale analysis of racial disparities in police stops across the United States," Working Paper, Stanford University, 2017, https://5harad.com/papers/traffic-stops.pdf

20. "Race and Wrongful Convictions in the United States," National Registry of Exonerations, March 7, 2017, http://www.law.umich.edu/special/exoneration/Documents/Race_and_Wrongful_Convictions.pdf

21. "Hearing on Reports of Racism in the Justice System of the United States," ACLU, October 27, 2014 https://www.aclu.org/sites/default/files/assets/141027_iachr_racial_disparities_aclu_submission_0.pdf

22. "Race and Wrongful Convictions in the United States," National Registry of Exonerations, March 7, 2017, http://www.law.umich.edu/special/exoneration/Documents/Race_and_Wrongful_Convictions.pdf

23. Barbara O'Brien and Catherine M. Grosso, "Report on Jury Selection Study," Digital Commons, Michigan State University College of Law, December 12, 2011, https://digitalcommons.law.msu.edu/cgi/viewcontent.cgi?referer=http://www.slate.com/articles/news_and_politics/crime/2015/08/racial_disparities_in_the_criminal_justice_system_eight_charts_illustrating.html&httpsredir=1&article=1330&context=facpubs

24. M. Marit Rehavi and Sonja B. Starr, "Racial Disparity in Federal Criminal Charging and Its Sentencing Consequences," University of Michigan Law & Economics, Empirical Legal Studies Center Paper No. 12-002, May 7, 2012, https://ssrn.com/abstract=1985377 or http://dx.doi.org/10.2139/ssrn.1985377

25. "Examining Racial and Ethnic Disparities in Probation Revocation: Summary Findings and Implications from a Multisite Study," Urban Institute, April 2014, https://www.urban.org/sites/default/files/publication/22746/413174-Examining-Racial-and-Ethnic-Disparities-in-Probation-Revocation.PDF

26. "Facts About Prisons and People in Prison," Sentencing Project, accessed March 2018, https://www.sentencingproject.org/wp-content/uploads/2016/02/Facts-About-Prisons.pdf

27. "America's Disappeared Black Men," Sentencing Project, accessed March 2018, https://www.sentencingproject.org/news/americas-disappeared-black-men

28. "Black Boys Viewed as Older, Less Innocent Than Whites, Research Finds," American Psychological Association, accessed March 2018, http://www.apa.org/news/press/releases/2014/03/black-boys-older.aspx

29. Rebecca Epstein, Jamilia J. Blake, and Thalia González, "Girlhood Interrupted: The Erasure of Black Girls' Childhood," Center on Poverty and Inequality Georgetown

Law, accessed March 2018, http://www.law.georgetown.edu/academics/centers-institutes/poverty-inequality/upload/girlhood-interrupted.pdf

30. "Juvenile Populations: 1990–2016," National Center for Juvenile Justice, accessed March 2018, https://www.ojjdp.gov/ojstatbb/ezapop/asp/profile_display.asp

31. "Black Disparities in Youth Incarceration," Sentencing Project, September 2017, https://www.sentencingproject.org/wp-content/uploads/2017/09/Black-Disparities-in-Youth-Incarceration.pdf

32. "Latino Disparities in Youth Incarceration," Sentencing Project, October 12, 2017, https://www.sentencingproject.org/publications/latino-disparities-youth-incarceration

33. Native Disparities in Youth Incarceration," Sentencing Project, October 12, 2017, https://www.sentencingproject.org/publications/native-disparities-youth-incarceration

Chapter 5

Wealth

1. Heather Koball, Yang Jiang, "Basic Facts about Low-Income Children: Children under 18 Years, 2016," National Center for Children in Poverty (NCCP), January 2018, http://www.nccp.org/publications/pub_1194.html

2. Peter Coy, "The Big Reason Whites Are Richer Than Blacks in America," Bloomberg, February, 08, 2017, https://www.bloomberg.com/news/articles/2017-02-08/the-big-reason-whites-are-richer-than-blacks-in-america

3. "Labor Force Statistics from the Current Population Survey," U.S. Bureau of Labor Statistics, accessed March 2018, https://www.bls.gov/web/empsit/cpsee_e16.htm

4. Hilary Hurd Anyaso, "Research finds entrenched hiring bias against African-Americans," Northwestern University, September 12, 2017, https://news.northwestern.edu/stories/2017/september/research-finds-entrenched-hiring-bias-against-african-americans

5. Zara Zhi, "Asian Woman's Viral Post Highlights Job Discrimination Based on Race," *AsAm News*, September 30, 2016, https://asamnews.com/2016/09/30/asian-womans-viral-post-highlights-job-discrimination-based-on-race

6. S. Malos, "Post-9/11 backlash in the workplace: Employer liability for discrimination against Arab- and Muslim-Americans based on religion or national origin," *Employee Responsibilities and Rights Journal*, 22(4), 297-310, 2010. http://dx.doi.org/10.1007/s10672-009-9132-4

7. Ariane Hegewisch and Emma Williams-Baron, "The Gender Wage Gap: 2016; Earnings Differences by Gender, Race, and Ethnicity," *Women's Policy Research*, September 13, 2017, https://iwpr.org/publications/gender-wage-gap-2016-earnings-differences-gender-race-ethnicity

8. Bernadette Proctor, Jessica L. Semega, and Melissa A. Kollar, "U.S. Census Bureau, Current Population Reports, P60-256 (RV), Income and Poverty in the United States 2015," U.S. Government Printing Office, Washington, DC, 2016.

9. Lauren Musu-Gillette, Jennifer Robinson, Joel McFarland, Angelina KewalRamani, Anlan Zhang, and Sidney Wilkinson-Flicker. "Status and Trends in the Education of Racial and Ethnic Groups 2016" (NCES 2016-007). U.S. Department of Education, National Center for Education Statistics, Washington, DC, 2016. Retrieved 2018 from http://nces.ed.gov/pubsearch.

10. Michael W. Kraus, Julian M. Rucker, and Jennifer A. Richeson. "Americans misperceive racial economic equality," *Proceedings of the National Academy of Sciences*, September 2017, 114 (39) 10324-10331; DOI:10.1073/pnas.1707719114

11. Angela Hanks, Danyelle Solomon, and Christian E. Weller, "Systematic Inequality," Center for American Progress, February 21, 2018, https://www.americanprogress.org/issues/race/reports/2018/02/21/447051/systematic-inequality

12. "Jim Crow Laws," History.com, accessed March 2018, https://www.history.com/topics/jim-crow-laws

13. Crystal N. Galyean, "Levittown: The Imperfect Rise of the American Suburbs," U.S. History Scene, April 10, 2015, http://ushistoryscene.com/article/levittown

14. "New Deal," History.com, accessed March 2018, https://www.history.com/topics/new-deal

15. "Historian Says Don't 'Sanitize' How Our Government Created Ghettos," National Public Radio (NPR), May 14, 2015, https://www.npr.org/templates/transcript/transcript.php?storyId=406699264

16. Paul Kiel with Hannah Fresques, "How the Bankruptcy System Is Failing Black Americans," ProPublica, September 27, 2017, https://features.propublica.org/bankruptcy-inequality/bankruptcy-failing-black-americans-debt-chapter-13

17. Nikole Hannah-Jones, "Have You Experienced Housing Discrimination?" ProPublica, October 28, 2012, https://www.propublica.org/getinvolved/have-you-experienced-housing-discrimination

Chapter 6

Health

1. H. Allcott, R. Diamond, and J.P. Dube, *The Geography of Poverty and Nutrition: Food Deserts and Food Choices Across the United States.* (National Bureau Of Economic Research, Cambridge, 2017) http://www.nber.org/papers/w24094

2. Alex Shashkevich, "Stanford scholar traces medical experimentation on slaves in 18th-century Caribbean colonies," Stanford University, August 10, 2017, https://news.stanford.edu/2017/08/10/medical-experimentation-slaves-18th-century-caribbean-colonies

3. Brynn Holland, "The 'Father of Modern Gynecology' Performed Shocking Experiments on Slaves," History.com, August 29, 2017, https://www.history.com/news/the-father-of-modern-gynecology-performed-shocking-experiments-on-slaves

4. Paul Lombardo, "Eugenic Sterilization Laws" Image Archive on the American Eugenics Movement, accessed March 2018, http://www.eugenicsarchive.org/html/eugenics/essay8text.html

5. Lisa Ko, "Unwanted Sterilization and Eugenics Programs in the United States," Public Broadcasting Service, January 29, 2016, http://www.pbs.org/independentlens/blog/unwanted-sterilization-and-eugenics-programs-in-the-united-states

6. "1976: Government admits forced sterilization of Indian Women," U.S. National Library of Medicine, accessed March 2018, https://www.nlm.nih.gov/nativevoices/timeline/543.html

7. "The Tuskegee Timeline," Centers for Disease Control and Prevention, accessed March 2018, https://www.cdc.gov/tuskegee/timeline.htm

8. "Reducing Disparities in the Federal Health Care Budget," National Congress of American Indians, accessed March 2018, http://www.ncai.org/policy-issues/tribal-governance/budget-and-approprations/07_FY2016_Health_NCAI_Budget.pdf

9. "Depression in Communities of Color," Public Broadcasting Service, https://www-tc.pbs.org/wgbh/takeonestep/depression/pdf/dep_color.pdf

10. Monique Tello, "Racism and discrimination in health care: Providers and patients," Harvard Health Publishing, January 16, 2017, https://www.health.harvard.edu/blog/racism-discrimination-health-care-providers-patients-2017011611015

11. Myra J. Tucker, Cynthia J. Berg, William M. Callaghan, and Jason Hsia, "The Black–White Disparity in Pregnancy-Related Mortality from 5 Conditions: Differences in Prevalence and Case-Fatality Rates," *American Journal of Public Health* 97, no. 2 (February 1, 2007): pp. 247-251. DOI: 10.2105/AJPH.2005.072975

12. "Infant Mortality Rate (Deaths per 1,000 Live Births) by Race/Ethnicity," Kaiser Family Foundation, accessed March 2018, https://www.kff.org/other/state-indicator/infant-mortality-rate-by-race-ethnicity

13. Eugene Scott, "Native Americans, among the most harmed by the opioid epidemic, are often left out of conversation," *Washington Post*, October 30, 2017, https://www.washingtonpost.com/news/the-fix/wp/2017/10/30/native-americans-among-the-most-harmed-by-the-opioid-epidemic-are-often-left-out-of-conversation/?utm_term=.de93685eb7e0

14. "The Oral Health Crisis Among Native Americans," Pew Charitable Trusts, July 23, 2015, http://www.pewtrusts.org/en/research-and-analysis/fact-sheets/2015/06/the-oral-health-crisis-among-native-americans

15. "Reducing Disparities in the Federal Health Care Budget," National Congress of American Indians, accessed March 2018, http://www.ncai.org/policy-issues/tribal-governance/budget-and-approprations/07_FY2016_Health_NCAI_Budget.pdf

16. "A timeline of the water crisis in Flint, Michigan," Associated Press, September 24, 2016, https://apnews.com/e6210d0001be4092943826c5381f0f13

17. Cynthia G. Colen, David M. Ramey, Elizabeth C. Cooksey, and David R. Williams, "Racial disparities in health among nonpoor African Americans and Hispanics: The role of acute and chronic discrimination," *Social Science & Medicine*, 2017, http://dx.doi.org/10.1016/j.socscimed.2017.04.051

18. Working Group on Stress and Health Disparities, "Stress and health disparities: Contexts, mechanisms, and interventions among racial/ethnic minority and low-socioeconomic status populations," American Psychological Association, 2017. Retrieved from http://www.apa.org/pi/health-disparities/resources/stress-report.aspx

Glossary

achievement gap The differences in grades, dropout rates, standardized test scores, course options, and college success experienced by different students.

American dream The belief that America is the land of opportunity where anyone can be successful.

bootstrap myth The false belief that persistence and hard work are enough to get you out of economic and other struggles.

domestic terrorism Crimes committed against one's fellow citizens, especially when done with political, religious, or social motives.

individual racism Direct denial of service, use of slurs, or intentional harm caused because of a person of color's race.

institutional racism When hateful mindsets (individual racism) are used to directly or indirectly have negative effects for people on color in various institutions.

people of color A term used to describe anyone who is not white/Euro-American, regardless of skin tone. Can also apply to biracial individuals.

property taxes Taxes that are paid on a home. This is one of the most common methods of school funding in public education.

race A concept that is supposed to explain differences in appearance, intelligence, social customs, and other factors. Typically indicated by physical qualities like skin color, hair texture, hue, and stature.

racial equity A reality where race doesn't change how likely you are to experience privileges or disadvantages in society.

racial profiling Accusing someone of a crime or offense based on their being a particular race or ethnicity.

racial wealth gap The unequal range between the wealth held by white Americans vs. people of color, caused by centuries of policies in favor of white people.

school-to-prison pipeline The combined effects of police presence in schools, unequal suspension/expulsion rate, and zero-tolerance policies that unequally affect children of color and filter them into the criminal justice system as early as preschool.

structural racism The normalized and legitimized range of policies, practices, and attitudes that routinely produce cumulative and chronic adverse outcomes for people of color.

Further Reading

Books

Wesley Lowery. *They Can't Kill Us All: Ferguson, Baltimore, and a New Era in America's Racial Justice Movement*. New York, NY: Little, Brown and Company, 2016.

Walter J. Nicholls. *The DREAMers: How the Undocumented Youth Movement Transformed the Immigrant Rights Debate*. Stanford, CA: (Stanford University Press, 2013.

Andrea J. Ritchie. *Invisible No More*. Boston, MA: Beacon Press, 2017.

Websites

Awareness Harmony Acceptance Advocates
http://Breakingprejudice.org/teaching/group-activities
This site in an excellent source for anyone looking for informative and interactive ways to learn more about various forms of racism and prejudice. It has group activities that help children inside and outside of the classroom.

Race: Are We So different?
http://www.understandingrace.org
This site provides a science-based explanation of race that helps all ages understand what race is, as well as how it affects daily life.

Unlearn Racism
http://unlearnracism.ca
This interactive site for children provides working definitions of race, ethnicity, and similar concepts while causing children to think critically about racism.

Index

A

achievement gap, 20-22
affirmative action programs, 12, 47
alt-right groups, 33-34
American Civil Liberties Union (ACLU), 63
American Indian Movement (AIM), 64
American Psychological Association, 62
Arizona Anti-Immigration Law (SB 1070), 38

B

Black Lives Matter (BLM), 64-65
Brown, Michael, 29
bullying, 5, 8-9

C

Civil Rights Act of 1964, 10
colorblind racism, 12
Couch, Ethan, 29
Cruz, Nikolas, 22-23, 36
cultural insensitivity, 6, 60, 62, 65

D

Dakota Access Pipeline, 38
Dear, Robert L., 36
Detroit, MI, 15-16, 17, 30
diabetes, 55
domestic terrorism, 28-29

E

education
    access to, 5, 7, 9, 10, 15-16, 19, 20, 21, 23, 27, 49, 61
    quality of, 15-16, 17, 18, 20, 24-25, 67
employment, 4, 5, 7, 10, 13, 17, 25, 44, 45, 46-49, 50-51, 52, 55, 61, 67
eugenics, 57
European Dissent, 65

F

Ferguson, MO, 29, 31
Flint, MI, 61

G

Gates, Henry Louis, 39

H

hair discrimination, 4, 14, 19
housing discrimination, 52-54
Hurricane Katrina (2005), 28

I

immigration, 31, 33
imprisonment, rate of, 24, 39, 41-43, 44
Indian Health Service, 57-58
Indian Removal Act, 38
individual racism, 5, 8-9, 48
institutional racism
    in the criminal justice system, 39, 41, 43
    definition, 5-7, 8-10
    in education, 24-25
    in employment, 48-49
    in health care, 55, 56, 60, 62
    in the media, 33-34

J

Jim Crow laws, 4, 51
Jones, Aiyana, 30

M

Marya, Rupa K., 58
mental illness, 27, 28